# 10 TIPS FOR BUILDING WEALTH IN YOUR 20S

DAMI JOSH

# TABLE OF CONTENT

# INTRODUCTION

Welcome to "10 Tips for Building Wealth in Your 20s," a comprehensive guide crafted to empower young adults on their journey to financial success. In a world of economic uncertainties, mastering the art of wealth-building early in life is not just a luxury; it's a necessity. This book is designed to be your roadmap, offering practical and actionable advice tailored to the unique challenges and opportunities that the twenties present.

As the author, I understand the pivotal role this decade plays in shaping one's financial future. The choices made in these formative years can set the stage for a lifetime of financial security or, conversely, financial stress. With a focus on Amazon, the global marketplace that mirrors the diversity of its users, these tips transcend borders and apply to anyone navigating the complex landscape of personal finance.

The book begins by laying the groundwork for financial literacy, emphasizing the importance of understanding basic concepts such as budgeting, saving, and investing. It then delves into the specifics, providing insights on identifying lucrative opportunities and avoiding common pitfalls. From leveraging technology to building a diversified investment portfolio, each tip is a building block for a solid financial foundation.

Moreover, the book addresses the psychological aspects of wealth-building, recognizing the impact of mindset and habits on financial outcomes. By merging practical strategies with a holistic approach, readers will gain not only the tools to accumulate wealth but also the mindset to sustain and grow it.

Whether you're a recent graduate, an aspiring entrepreneur, or someone seeking to take control of your financial destiny, "10 Tips for Building Wealth in Your 20s" is your go-to guide. Let's embark on this transformative journey together, unlocking the secrets to financial success and building a prosperous future.

# 7 | 10 TIPS FOR BUILDING WEALTH IN YOUR 20S

# CHAPTER 1: FINANCIAL FOUNDATIONS IN YOUR 20S

Welcome to "Financial Foundations in Your 20s," the pivotal opening chapter of our guide to building wealth during this transformative decade of life. As you stand on the threshold of adulthood, the decisions you make now will profoundly shape your financial trajectory. This chapter serves as a compass, guiding you through the essential principles and practices that form the bedrock of financial success.

In these initial pages, we embark on a journey of financial literacy, recognizing that a strong understanding of foundational concepts is paramount. We'll delve into the nuts and bolts of personal finance, demystifying topics such as budgeting, saving, and emergency fund creation. Whether you're a recent graduate entering the workforce or an ambitious entrepreneur navigating the complexities of financial management, this chapter provides a solid groundwork to ensure that your financial house is built on a sturdy foundation.

We kick off by demystifying the jargon, ensuring that you not only understand the terminology but also feel confident in applying these concepts to your unique financial situation. From creating a budget that aligns with your goals to establishing emergency funds for unforeseen circumstances, these practical insights lay the groundwork for responsible financial management.

As we navigate through "Financial Foundations in Your 20s," remember that this chapter is more than a set of guidelines; it's an invitation to empower yourself with the knowledge necessary to make informed financial decisions. By mastering these foundational elements, you'll not only weather the financial challenges that may arise but also position yourself for future success as we explore the subsequent chapters of this wealth-building journey. Let's commence our exploration, setting the stage for a financially prosperous future.

# - Basic Financial Concepts

In the journey toward financial empowerment during your twenties, a solid grasp of basic financial concepts is the cornerstone of success. This chapter aims to demystify the fundamental principles that govern personal finance, providing you with the knowledge needed to navigate the complexities of the financial world.

1. **Income and Expenses:** Start by comprehending the dynamics of your income and expenses. Learn to distinguish between gross and net income, and understand how to allocate your resources effectively to cover necessities, discretionary spending, and savings.

2. **Budgeting:** Creating a budget is more than just tracking expenses; it's a strategic tool for financial management. This section guides you through the process of crafting a realistic budget that aligns with your financial goals, emphasizing the importance of prioritizing needs over wants.

3. **Saving Strategies:** Delve into the art of saving, exploring various strategies to build a financial cushion. From short-term goals like vacations to long-term objectives like homeownership or retirement, discover how to allocate your savings across different buckets.

4. **Debt Management:** Understand the implications of debt and how to manage it responsibly. Differentiate between good and bad debt, and explore strategies to pay down outstanding balances efficiently while avoiding common pitfalls.

5. **Credit Scores:** Unravel the mysteries of credit scores and reports. Learn how your creditworthiness impacts your financial life, and discover actionable steps to build and maintain a healthy credit profile.

By the end of this chapter, you'll not only have a clear understanding of these basic financial concepts but also possess the skills to apply them in your day-to-day life. Armed with this knowledge, you'll be better equipped to make informed financial decisions and lay the groundwork for a secure and prosperous future.

## - Creating and Managing a Budget

Creating and managing a budget is a fundamental skill that forms the backbone of responsible financial stewardship. This process empowers you to take control of your money, allocate resources effectively, and work towards your financial goals. Let's delve into the key steps involved in creating and managing a budget:

1. **Income Assessment:**

- Begin by assessing your income. Identify all sources of income, including your salary, freelance work, side hustles, or any other monetary inflows.

## 2. Expense Categorization:

- Break down your expenses into categories. Common categories include housing, utilities, groceries, transportation, debt payments, entertainment, and savings. This categorization provides a comprehensive overview of your spending patterns.

## 3. Determine Fixed and Variable Expenses:

- Differentiate between fixed and variable expenses. Fixed expenses, such as rent or mortgage payments, remain constant, while variable expenses, like dining out or entertainment, can fluctuate. Understanding this distinction is crucial for effective budgeting.

## 4. Set Financial Goals:

- Define short-term and long-term financial goals. Whether it's building an emergency fund, paying off debt, or saving for a vacation, having clear objectives will guide your budgeting decisions.

### 5. **Allocate Funds:**

- Allocate your income to cover your expenses and contribute to your financial goals. Prioritize essential needs such as housing, utilities, and debt payments before assigning funds to discretionary spending.

### 6. **Emergency Fund:**

- Allocate a portion of your budget to building and maintaining an emergency fund. This financial safety net provides a cushion for unexpected expenses, preventing you from derailing your financial plan.

### 7. **Regularly Track and Adjust:**

- Budgeting is an ongoing process. Regularly track your spending against your budget, identifying areas where adjustments may be needed. This flexibility ensures that your budget remains realistic and adaptable to changes in your financial situation.

8. **Utilize Budgeting Tools:**

   - Leverage technology to streamline the budgeting process. Various apps and tools can help you track expenses, set financial goals, and provide insights into your spending habits.

9. **Review and Reflect:**

   - Periodically review your budget to assess your progress towards financial goals. Reflect on your achievements and challenges, adjusting your budget as needed to stay on course.

Creating and managing a budget is not a one-size-fits-all endeavor. It's a dynamic process that evolves with your life circumstances. By mastering this skill in your twenties, you lay the groundwork for a financially sound future, equipped to handle both planned expenses and unexpected financial challenges.

# - Establishing Emergency Funds

Building an emergency fund is a crucial step in achieving financial stability and resilience. This financial safety net serves as a buffer against unexpected expenses or sudden changes in income. Here's a comprehensive guide to establishing and maintaining an emergency fund:

1. **Set a Target Amount:**

   - Determine the ideal size for your emergency fund. Financial experts often recommend saving three to six months' worth of living expenses. This amount provides a substantial cushion to cover unforeseen circumstances without significantly impacting your financial stability.

2. **Calculate Living Expenses:**

- Assess your monthly living expenses, including rent or mortgage, utilities, groceries, insurance, and other necessities. This calculation serves as the baseline for your emergency fund target.

### 3. **Start Small, Be Consistent:**

- If the thought of saving a large sum is daunting, start small. Consistency is key. Begin by setting aside a manageable amount from each paycheck and gradually increase it as your financial situation improves.

### 4. **Automate Savings:**

- Simplify the process by automating your savings. Set up an automatic transfer to your emergency fund each month. Treating it as a non-negotiable expense ensures that you prioritize building your financial safety net.

### 5. **Choose a Separate Account:**

- Keep your emergency fund separate from your regular spending accounts. Consider opening a dedicated savings account or utilizing a separate section within your existing account. This separation helps prevent impulsive spending while preserving the fund's intended purpose.

## 6. Utilize Windfalls:

- Direct unexpected windfalls, such as tax refunds, work bonuses, or monetary gifts, towards your emergency fund. This accelerates the growth of your fund without impacting your regular budget.

## 7. Avoid Tapping into the Fund Unnecessarily:

- Reserve your emergency fund for genuine emergencies. Avoid the temptation to dip into it for non-essential expenses. Maintaining discipline ensures that the fund remains robust when needed.

## 8. Regularly Assess and Adjust:

- Periodically reassess your financial situation and adjust your emergency fund target as needed. Life changes, such as job transitions or changes in living expenses, may necessitate modifications to your savings goals.

## 9. **Replenish After Use:**

- If you need to tap into your emergency fund, make it a priority to replenish it. Swift replenishment ensures that your financial safety net is always ready for the next unexpected challenge.

## 10. **Review and Celebrate Milestones:**

- Celebrate milestones in your emergency fund journey. Whether it's reaching a certain dollar amount or maintaining consistent contributions, acknowledging your progress reinforces positive financial habits.

Establishing an emergency fund is an investment in your financial peace of mind. By diligently following these steps, you fortify your financial foundation, allowing you to face life's uncertainties with confidence and resilience.

# CHAPTER 2: INVESTING 101: NAVIGATING THE WORLD OF FINANCE

Welcome to "Investing 101: Navigating the World of Finance," a chapter designed to demystify the intricate landscape of investment and empower you to make informed decisions that lay the groundwork for long-term financial growth. As you navigate through your twenties, understanding the fundamentals of investing becomes paramount in building wealth and securing your financial future.

In this chapter, we embark on a journey into the core principles of investing, offering insights that cater to both novices and those looking to refine their investment strategies. The world of finance can be intimidating, but armed with knowledge, you can harness the potential for your financial benefit.

We begin by unravelling the basics and exploring what it means to invest and the various avenues available. From stocks and bonds to alternative investment vehicles, we'll break down these concepts into digestible, actionable insights. Understanding risk and return dynamics is key, and we'll guide you through assessing your risk tolerance and setting realistic investment goals.

As we navigate through "Investing 101," we'll delve into the importance of building a diversified investment portfolio. The adage "don't put all your eggs in one basket" holds, and we'll explore strategies to spread risk intelligently across different asset classes.

Moreover, we'll discuss the role of time in investment success. Time is a powerful ally in the world of finance, and we'll uncover the principles of compounding and long-term wealth accumulation. Whether you're considering investing in individual stocks, mutual funds, or other investment vehicles, this chapter provides a roadmap for making strategic decisions aligned with your financial objectives.

Investing is not solely about numbers and market trends; it also involves understanding your values and aligning your investments with them. Socially responsible investing and ethical considerations are becoming increasingly important, and we'll explore how you can invest with both profit and purpose.

So, let's embark on this journey through the realm of investing. By the end of this chapter, you'll be equipped with the knowledge and confidence to navigate the world of finance, making strategic investment decisions that propel you towards financial prosperity in your twenties and beyond.

## - Investing Principles

Entering the realm of investing can be both exciting and daunting. "Introduction to Investing Principles" serves as your foundational guide, illuminating the essential concepts that underpin successful investment strategies. In this chapter, we demystify the jargon, clarify key principles, and empower you to navigate the complexities of the financial markets with confidence.

## 1. Understanding the Purpose of Investing:

- Begin by grasping the fundamental purpose of investing. Whether your goal is wealth accumulation, retirement planning, or achieving specific financial milestones, clarity on your objectives sets the stage for strategic decision-making.

## 2. Risk and Return Dynamics:

- Delve into the critical relationship between risk and return. Learn how different asset classes carry varying levels of risk and potential reward. This understanding is pivotal in aligning your investment choices with your risk tolerance and financial goals.

## 3. Time Horizon and Compounding:

- Explore the concept of time as a crucial factor in investment success. Understand how compounding works to amplify returns over time, emphasizing the importance of a long-term perspective in building wealth.

## 4. Asset Allocation:

- Grasp the significance of asset allocation in constructing a well-balanced investment portfolio. Learn how diversifying across asset classes—such as stocks, bonds, and alternative investments—can mitigate risk and enhance overall portfolio stability.

## 5. Research and Due Diligence:

- Develop the skills of thorough research and due diligence before making investment decisions. From analyzing individual stocks to evaluating mutual funds, understanding the fundamentals and potential risks of your chosen investments is key to making informed choices.

## 6. Market Volatility and Emotional Discipline:

- Acknowledge the inevitability of market fluctuations and the emotional discipline required to navigate them. Develop strategies to stay focused on your long-term goals amid market volatility and avoid reactionary decision-making.

**7. Costs and Fees:**

   - Uncover the impact of costs and fees on your investment returns. Whether its transaction fees, management fees, or expense ratios, being aware of these costs ensures that you maximize the returns on your investments.

**8. Stay Informed and Adaptive:**

   - Recognize the dynamic nature of financial markets and the importance of staying informed. Develop a habit of continuous learning, keeping abreast of economic trends, market developments, and emerging investment opportunities.

By the conclusion of this chapter, you'll have gained a comprehensive understanding of these fundamental investing principles. Armed with this knowledge, you'll be better equipped to formulate a well-informed investment strategy that aligns with your financial objectives and risk tolerance. As we navigate the intricate world of finance, these principles will serve as your compass, guiding you toward investment success.

# - Types of Investments: Stocks, Bonds, and Beyond

As you embark on your investment journey, understanding the diverse landscape of investment options is pivotal. "Types of Investments: Stocks, Bonds, and Beyond" is a comprehensive exploration of the major asset classes, providing insights into the characteristics, risks, and potential rewards associated with each.

1. **Stocks:**

   - Delve into the world of equities, or stocks, which represent ownership in a company. Learn about the potential for capital appreciation as stock values rise, the influence of dividends, and the inherent volatility of individual stocks. Discover strategies for selecting stocks aligned with your investment goals.

## 2. **Bonds:**

- Explore the fixed-income side of investments with bonds. Understand how bonds represent debt issued by governments, municipalities, or corporations. Learn about coupon payments, maturity dates, and the inverse relationship between bond prices and interest rates. Bonds are often considered more stable than stocks and can play a crucial role in diversifying a portfolio.

## 3. **Mutual Funds:**

- Uncover the benefits of mutual funds, which pool money from multiple investors to invest in a diversified portfolio of stocks, bonds, or other securities. Explore the advantages of professional fund management and the potential for broad market exposure. Understand different types of mutual funds, including equity funds, bond funds, and index funds.

## 4. Exchange-Traded Funds (ETFs):

- Navigate the world of ETFs, investment funds that are traded on stock exchanges. Understand the similarities and differences between ETFs and mutual funds, as well as the advantages of ETFs in terms of liquidity, transparency, and cost-effectiveness. Explore how ETFs can provide exposure to specific sectors, commodities, or international markets.

## 5. Real Estate Investments:

- Broaden your investment horizon by exploring real estate. Learn about the potential for capital appreciation, rental income, and diversification that real estate investments offer. Understand the various ways to invest in real estate, from direct property ownership to Real Estate Investment Trusts (REITs).

## 6. Cryptocurrencies and Alternative Investments:

- Step into the realm of alternative investments, including cryptocurrencies like Bitcoin and Ethereum. Understand the unique characteristics, risks, and potential rewards associated with these assets. Explore how alternative investments can add diversity to a portfolio but also require a thorough understanding and careful consideration.

7. **Commodities:**

- Explore the world of commodities, including physical goods like gold, silver, oil, and agricultural products. Understand the role of commodities as a hedge against inflation and how they can contribute to a well-rounded investment portfolio.

This chapter aims to provide you with a comprehensive overview of various investment options, allowing you to make informed decisions based on your financial goals, risk tolerance, and investment horizon. Diversifying your portfolio across different asset classes can enhance stability and optimize returns, creating a well-balanced and resilient investment strategy.

# - Building a Diversified Investment Portfolio

Constructing a diversified investment portfolio is akin to assembling a well-balanced financial ecosystem that can weather market fluctuations and enhance overall stability. This strategic approach involves spreading investments across different asset classes to optimize returns while mitigating risk. Here's a step-by-step guide to building a diversified investment portfolio:

1. **Define Your Investment Goals and Risk Tolerance:**

   - Start by clearly defining your investment objectives. Whether it's wealth accumulation, retirement planning, or a specific financial goal, understanding your aims is crucial. Additionally, assess your risk tolerance – the level of market volatility you can endure without abandoning your long-term strategy.

## 2. Understand Asset Classes:

- Familiarize yourself with various asset classes, such as stocks, bonds, real estate, and commodities. Each class carries distinct risk and return characteristics. Understanding these differences is foundational to effective diversification.

## 3. Allocate Across Asset Classes:

- Based on your goals and risk tolerance, allocate your investment capital across different asset classes. For example, a mix of stocks and bonds can provide a balance of growth potential and stability. The specific allocation will vary based on your circumstances.

## 4. Diversify Within Asset Classes:

- Within each asset class, further diversify to minimize risk. For stocks, consider diversifying across industries and geographic regions. For bonds, explore different maturities and credit qualities.

This intra-asset diversification hedges against the specific risks associated with individual securities.

## 5. Consider Mutual Funds and ETFs:

   - Mutual funds and Exchange-Traded Funds (ETFs) are efficient vehicles for diversification. These investment vehicles pool funds from multiple investors to create diversified portfolios. Explore funds that align with your investment goals, whether they focus on broad market indices, specific sectors, or geographic regions.

## 6. Include Real Assets:

   - Integrate real assets like real estate and commodities into your portfolio. Real assets often have a low correlation with traditional financial assets, providing an additional layer of diversification. Real Estate Investment Trusts (REITs) and commodity-focused ETFs are accessible options.

## 7. Rebalance Periodically:

- Regularly review and rebalance your portfolio to maintain the desired asset allocation. Market fluctuations can cause your portfolio to deviate from your initial allocation. Rebalancing involves selling assets that have appreciated significantly and reallocating funds to those that may be underrepresented.

## 8. Stay Informed and Adapt:

- Keep yourself informed about market trends, economic conditions, and shifts in the investment landscape. Be prepared to adapt your portfolio based on changes in your financial situation, market dynamics, or alterations in your investment goals.

## 9. Avoid Overconcentration:

- Guard against overconcentration in a single asset class or investment. While focusing on high-conviction investments is essential, an over concentrated portfolio can amplify risk. Diversification is about spreading risk intelligently.

Building a diversified investment portfolio is a dynamic and ongoing process. By following these steps, you create a resilient financial strategy that adapts to changing market conditions while working towards your long-term financial goals. Remember, a well-diversified portfolio not only seeks returns but also prioritizes risk management for a balanced and sustainable investment approach.

# CHAPTER 3: LEVERAGING TECHNOLOGY FOR FINANCIAL GROWTH

Welcome to "Leveraging Technology for Financial Growth," a chapter that explores the intersection of finance and technology to empower you in your quest for financial success. In an era where technological advancements are reshaping every aspect of our lives, harnessing these tools can be a game-changer in your journey to build wealth and financial security.

This chapter is a roadmap to understanding how cutting-edge technologies can be leveraged to enhance your financial decision-making, streamline processes, and open up new avenues for growth. From budgeting apps that bring financial management to your fingertips to sophisticated investment platforms that democratize access to the market, technology is reshaping the landscape of personal finance.

We will delve into the practical applications of technology across various facets of financial management, demonstrating how these tools can be harnessed to optimize budgeting, automate savings, and navigate the complexities of investing. Moreover, the chapter will explore the role of artificial intelligence, machine learning, and data analytics in providing insights that were once reserved for financial experts.

As we journey through "Leveraging Technology for Financial Growth," you'll discover how fintech innovations can empower you to take control of your financial destiny. Whether you're a tech-savvy young professional or someone seeking to embrace digital tools for the first time, this chapter is designed to demystify the tech-driven financial landscape and provide actionable insights that align with the unique challenges and opportunities of the digital age.

Get ready to explore the transformative potential of technology in shaping your financial future. By the end of this chapter, you'll be equipped with the knowledge and tools to navigate the digital realm of personal finance, leveraging technology to propel your financial growth in innovative and unprecedented ways.

## - The Role of Technology in Personal Finance

In the rapidly evolving landscape of personal finance, technology plays a pivotal role, reshaping the way individuals manage, track, and optimize their financial lives. This integration of technology into personal finance has democratized access to information, streamlined processes, and empowered individuals to take control of their financial destinies. Here's a closer look at the multifaceted role of technology in personal finance:

1. **Budgeting and Expense Tracking Apps:**

- Budgeting is the cornerstone of sound financial management, and technology has brought this process to the palm of your hand. Apps like Mint, YNAB (You Need A Budget), and PocketGuard enable users to create, track, and manage budgets effortlessly. These tools categorize expenses, provide real-time spending insights, and offer proactive alerts, fostering financial discipline.

2. **Automated Savings and Investment Platforms:**

- Technology has revolutionized savings and investing by automating these processes. Robo-advisors, such as Wealthfront and Betterment, leverage algorithms to create and manage diversified investment portfolios based on users' financial goals and risk tolerance. Automated savings apps, like Acorns, round up everyday purchases to invest spare change, promoting a consistent savings habit.

### 3. Online Banking and Digital Wallets:

- Traditional banking has transformed with the advent of online banking services and digital wallets. These platforms allow users to manage their finances, transfer funds, and make payments seamlessly. Digital wallets, such as Apple Pay and Google Pay, provide secure and convenient ways to make transactions using mobile devices.

### 4. Cryptocurrencies and Blockchain Technology:

- Cryptocurrencies, powered by blockchain technology, have introduced new dimensions to personal finance. Bitcoin, Ethereum, and other cryptocurrencies offer decentralized and borderless alternatives for transactions and investments. Blockchain's transparency and security contribute to the evolution of financial systems.

**5. Personal Finance Education Platforms:**

- Technology has democratized access to financial education. Platforms like Investopedia, Khan Academy, and Coursera provide online courses and resources, empowering individuals to enhance their financial literacy. These tools offer insights into investing, budgeting, and various financial instruments.

**6. Credit Score Monitoring Apps:**

- Monitoring and understanding credit scores is essential for financial health. Apps like Credit Karma and Credit Sesame provide users with real-time updates on their credit scores, offer personalized tips for improvement, and educate users on the factors influencing their creditworthiness.

**7. AI-Powered Financial Insights:**

- Artificial Intelligence (AI) is increasingly employed to analyze financial data, providing personalized insights and recommendations. AI-driven financial advisors, such as chatbots and virtual assistants, offer tailored advice, answer queries, and guide users through financial decisions.

8. **Expense Analysis and Data Visualization:**

   - Data analytics tools allow users to analyze their spending patterns, identify trends, and make data-driven financial decisions. Visualizing financial data through charts and graphs enhances comprehension and facilitates strategic planning.

In essence, the integration of technology into personal finance is a transformative force, democratizing financial tools and knowledge. By embracing these innovations, individuals can optimize their financial strategies, make informed decisions, and cultivate a secure and prosperous financial future. The role of technology in personal finance is dynamic, continually evolving to meet the diverse needs of users in an increasingly digital and interconnected world.

## - Utilizing Budgeting Apps and Financial Tools

In the digital age, the power to take control of your finances is at your fingertips, thanks to the proliferation of budgeting apps and financial tools. These technological solutions offer real-time insights, automation, and user-friendly interfaces to streamline the budgeting process. Here's a step-by-step guide to effectively utilize these tools for better financial management:

1. **Research and Choose the Right App:**

   - Begin by researching and selecting a budgeting app or financial tool that aligns with your needs and preferences. Popular choices include Mint, YNAB (You Need A Budget), PocketGuard, and EveryDollar. Consider factors such as compatibility with your devices, user interface, and features offered.

## 2. Link Your Financial Accounts:

  - Once you've chosen an app, link it to your financial accounts. This includes bank accounts, credit cards, investment accounts, and any other accounts relevant to your financial situation. This linkage allows the app to pull in transaction data automatically.

## 3. Establish Budget Categories:

  - Set up budget categories based on your spending patterns. Common categories include housing, utilities, groceries, transportation, entertainment, and savings. Tailor these categories to match your unique lifestyle and financial goals.

## 4. Set Realistic Budget Limits:

  - Establish realistic budget limits for each category. Utilize insights from previous spending habits to guide your allocations. These limits serve as benchmarks, helping you stay within your financial boundaries.

## 5. Monitor and Categorize Transactions:

- Regularly monitor your transactions through the app. Most budgeting tools categorize transactions automatically, but it's essential to review and adjust categories as needed. This ensures accurate tracking and provides a real-time snapshot of your spending.

## 6. Utilize Automation Features:

- Take advantage of automation features offered by budgeting apps. Automatic transaction categorization, bill reminders, and goal tracking are examples of features that can streamline your financial management process, saving you time and reducing manual effort.

## 7. Create and Track Financial Goals:

- Set financial goals within the app. Whether it's saving for a vacation, building an emergency fund, or paying off debt, these tools can help you visualize progress and stay motivated. Regularly track your goal-related transactions to ensure you're on the right path.

8. **Review Reports and Insights:**

- Budgeting apps often provide insightful reports and analytics. Review these regularly to gain a deeper understanding of your spending habits, identify trends, and make informed decisions about your financial strategy.

9. **Adjust and Adapt:**

- Your financial situation may change over time, and your budget should adapt accordingly. Regularly reassess your budget, making adjustments to accommodate changes in income, expenses, or financial goals. Flexibility is key to long-term budgeting success.

10. **Secure Your Information:**

- Prioritize the security of your financial information. Choose apps with robust security measures, enable multi-factor authentication, and regularly update passwords to safeguard your sensitive data.

By following these steps, you can harness the full potential of budgeting apps and financial tools to gain control over your finances. The integration of technology into your budgeting process not only simplifies the management of your financial life but also empowers you with insights and tools to make informed decisions on your journey toward financial success.

# - Exploring Online Investment Platforms

In the digital era, online investment platforms have democratized access to financial markets, enabling individuals to invest in a diverse range of assets with ease. Whether you're a novice investor or a seasoned pro, exploring these platforms can open up new opportunities for wealth creation. Here's a comprehensive guide to navigating the process:

1. **Define Your Investment Goals:**

   - Begin by clearly defining your investment objectives. Whether you're saving for retirement, a major purchase, or simply seeking to grow your wealth, having a clear goal will guide your platform selection and investment strategy.

2. **Research and Compare Platforms:**

   - Conduct thorough research on different online investment platforms. Consider factors such as fees, available investment options, user interface, customer service, and educational resources. Popular platforms include Vanguard, Fidelity, Charles Schwab, Robinhood, and ETRADE.

3. **Understand Account Types:**

   - Online investment platforms offer various account types, each with its tax implications and benefits. Common types include Individual Retirement Accounts (IRAs), Roth IRAs, taxable brokerage accounts, and more. Choose the account type that aligns with your financial goals and tax situation.

## 4. **Evaluate Investment Options:**

- Assess the range of investment options offered by each platform. Some platforms specialize in exchange-traded funds (ETFs), while others provide access to individual stocks, bonds, mutual funds, and even alternative investments. Ensure the platform aligns with your preferred investment strategy.

## 5. **Consider Risk Tolerance and Diversification:**

- Before making investment decisions, evaluate your risk tolerance and the importance of diversification. Online platforms often provide risk assessment tools to help guide your choices.

Diversifying your portfolio across different asset classes mitigates risk and enhances stability.

6. **Review Fee Structures:**

- Understand the fee structures associated with each platform. Fees can include account maintenance fees, transaction fees, and management fees for certain funds. Choose a platform with transparent and competitive fees that align with your investment style.

7. **Utilize Educational Resources:**

- Take advantage of the educational resources provided by online investment platforms. Many platforms offer webinars, articles, and tutorials to help users understand investing concepts, market trends, and portfolio management strategies.

8. **Open and Fund Your Account:**

- Once you've chosen a platform, follow the account opening process. This typically involves providing personal information, selecting account types, and agreeing to terms and conditions. Fund your account through bank transfers or other accepted methods.

## 9. **Start Small and Learn:**

- If you're new to investing, consider starting with a small amount to familiarize yourself with the platform and the dynamics of the market. Learning by doing is a valuable approach in the world of investing.

## 10. **Monitor and Adjust:**

- Regularly monitor your investments and the performance of your portfolio. Online platforms provide tools and dashboards to track your holdings and assess overall performance. Be prepared to adjust your investment strategy as needed based on market conditions and changes in your financial situation.

Exploring online investment platforms is a dynamic and ongoing process. By taking a thoughtful and informed approach, you can leverage these platforms to build a diversified portfolio aligned with your financial goals. As technology continues to shape the financial landscape, online investment platforms remain valuable tools for individuals seeking to take control of their financial futures.

# CHAPTER 4: IDENTIFYING LUCRATIVE OPPORTUNITIES

Welcome to the chapter on "Identifying Lucrative Opportunities," where we embark on a journey to uncover pathways to financial growth and explore avenues that have the potential to yield significant returns. In the dynamic landscape of personal finance, recognizing and capitalizing on lucrative opportunities can be a transformative step towards building wealth in your 20s.

This chapter is designed to be your guide through the entrepreneurial landscape, gig economy, and various avenues for additional income. In an era defined by innovation and a gig-centric economy, the opportunities are diverse, spanning from traditional side hustles to groundbreaking entrepreneurial ventures. Whether you're seeking to supplement your income, pay off student loans, or lay the foundation for financial independence, this chapter provides insights and strategies to help you identify and seize these opportunities.

We'll explore the principles of identifying lucrative opportunities, assess the skills and resources you bring to the table, and discuss various avenues that align with your interests and goals. From freelancing and consulting to launching your own business, we'll navigate the landscape of possibilities, offering practical advice and inspiring stories to fuel your entrepreneurial spirit.

So, if you're ready to unlock your potential, dive into the exploration of opportunities that extend beyond the conventional, and discover how your unique skills and passions can translate into financial success, this chapter is your gateway. Let's embark on this journey together, unravelling the threads of opportunity that have the potential to reshape your financial landscape and set you on the path to prosperity in your 20s and beyond.

# - Capitalizing on Side Hustles and Freelancing

In the dynamic landscape of the gig economy, side hustles and freelancing have emerged as powerful avenues for individuals to diversify their income streams and capitalize on their skills and passions. Whether you're looking to boost your earnings, pay off debts, or invest in your future, engaging in side hustles and freelancing can be a strategic step. Here's a comprehensive guide to help you navigate and capitalize on these opportunities:

1. Identify Your Skills and Passions:

   - Start by identifying your skills, talents, and passions. What are you good at, and what do you enjoy doing? This self-awareness is crucial in selecting side hustles or freelance gigs that align with your abilities and interests.

2. **Explore the Gig Economy Platforms:**

- Leverage gig economy platforms that connect freelancers with clients seeking specific services. Platforms like Upwork, Fiverr, and TaskRabbit cover a wide range of skills, from graphic design and writing to virtual assistance and handyman services. Create a compelling profile highlighting your expertise and experience.

3. **Set Clear Goals and Expectations:**

- Define your financial goals and expectations from your side hustle or freelancing endeavors. Whether it's earning extra income each month, saving for a specific goal, or transitioning to a full-time freelance career, clarity on your objectives guides your efforts.

4. **Establish a Professional Online Presence:**

- Create a professional online presence to showcase your skills and attract potential clients. Develop a personal website or utilize professional networking platforms like LinkedIn to build credibility and visibility within your industry.

## 5. **Network and Build Relationships:**

- Networking is crucial in the world of freelancing. Engage with potential clients, industry peers, and relevant communities. Word-of-mouth referrals and positive client relationships can significantly contribute to the success and growth of your side hustle.

## 6. **Price Your Services Strategically:**

- Determine fair and competitive pricing for your services. Consider your skill level, industry rates, and the value you bring to clients. Be transparent about your pricing structure to build trust with potential clients.

## 7. **Manage Your Time Effectively:**

- Balancing a side hustle with other commitments requires effective time management. Create a schedule that allows you to dedicate focused time to your freelancing activities. Set realistic deadlines and communicate clearly with clients about your availability.

## 8. **Invest in Skill Development:**

- Stay competitive by continually investing in your skill development. The freelance landscape evolves, and keeping your skills up-to-date enhances your marketability. Explore online courses, attend workshops, and participate in relevant industry events.

## 9. **Diversify Your Income Streams:**

- Consider diversifying your income streams by exploring different side hustles or freelancing niches. This not only maximizes your earning potential but also provides resilience against market fluctuations.

## 10. **Track Finances and Save for Taxes:**

- Keep meticulous records of your income and expenses. As a freelancer, you're responsible for managing your taxes, so set aside a portion of your earnings for tax payments. Utilize accounting tools or consult with a professional to ensure compliance.

By following these steps, you can effectively capitalize on side hustles and freelancing opportunities, turning your skills into a lucrative source of income. Whether you're looking for short-term financial gains or aiming to build a sustainable freelancing career, the gig economy offers a wealth of possibilities for those ready to seize them.

## - Entrepreneurial Ventures: From Idea to Execution

Embarking on an entrepreneurial venture is a thrilling and challenging journey that involves turning a vision into a viable business. The process, from conceiving an idea to executing a successful business plan, requires strategic planning, resilience, and a keen understanding of market dynamics. Here's a comprehensive guide on navigating the path from idea to execution:

**1. Ideation and Market Research:**

   - Begin by identifying a business idea that aligns with your passions and addresses a market need. Conduct thorough market research to understand your target audience, competition, and industry trends. This step lays the foundation for a viable and marketable concept.

**2. Define Your Value Proposition:**

   - Clearly articulate the value your product or service offers to customers. What sets your venture apart from competitors? Your value proposition should resonate with your target audience and solve a problem or fulfil a need they have.

### 3. Create a Business Plan:

- Develop a comprehensive business plan outlining your venture's goals, target market, revenue model, marketing strategy, and financial projections. A well-crafted business plan not only serves as a roadmap but also enhances your ability to secure funding and partnerships.

### 4. Assess Funding Options:

- Evaluate funding options to bring your entrepreneurial venture to life. Whether through personal savings, loans, angel investors, venture capital, or crowdfunding, choose the funding model that aligns with your business needs and growth plans.

### 5. Build a Prototype or Minimum Viable Product (MVP):

- Depending on your business type, create a prototype or MVP to demonstrate the functionality and value of your product. This initial version allows you to gather feedback, refine your offering, and validate its market potential.

6. **Establish a Legal Structure:**

   - Choose a legal structure for your business, such as a sole proprietorship, LLC, or corporation. Consider legal and regulatory requirements, tax implications, and the level of liability protection you need. Consult with legal professionals to ensure compliance.

7. **Build Your Brand:**

   - Develop a strong brand identity that communicates your venture's values and resonates with your target audience. This includes designing a compelling logo, establishing an online presence, and creating a consistent brand message.

8. **Launch and Market Strategically:**

   - Strategically launch your venture, utilizing a mix of online and offline marketing channels. Leverage social media, content marketing, SEO, and other tactics to build awareness and attract your first customers. Monitor and adapt your marketing strategy based on performance metrics.

9. **Iterate Based on Feedback:**

  - Collect and analyze customer feedback continuously. Use this input to refine your product or service, enhance user experience, and address any pain points. An iterative approach ensures that your venture remains adaptable and aligned with customer needs.

10. **Scale and Diversify:**

  - Once your venture gains traction, explore opportunities for scaling and diversification. Consider expanding your product line, entering new markets, or forming strategic partnerships. This phase involves strategic decision-making to sustain and grow your entrepreneurial venture.

From ideation to execution, the journey of building an entrepreneurial venture is dynamic and filled with learning opportunities. By embracing the challenges and leveraging your creativity and determination, you can navigate the complexities of entrepreneurship and turn your idea into a thriving and sustainable business.

# - Navigating the Gig Economy

The gig economy, characterized by short-term and freelance work arrangements, offers individuals unprecedented flexibility and opportunities for diverse income streams. Navigating this dynamic landscape involves strategic planning, adaptability, and a keen understanding of your skills and market demands. Here's a comprehensive guide to help you successfully navigate the gig economy:

1. **Self-Assessment and Skill Identification:**

   - Begin by conducting a thorough self-assessment to identify your skills, strengths, and areas for improvement. This process will help you align your abilities with the demands of the gig economy.

## 2. Research and Explore Opportunities:

- Research the gig economy platforms relevant to your skills and interests. Platforms like Upwork, TaskRabbit, Uber, and Etsy cater to a wide range of talents and services. Explore multiple platforms to maximize your exposure to potential gigs.

## 3. Build a Strong Online Presence:

- Establish a professional online presence to showcase your skills and attract potential clients or customers. Create a compelling profile on gig economy platforms, and consider developing a personal website or leveraging social media to enhance your visibility.

## 4. Set Clear Goals and Objectives:

- Define your goals and objectives in the gig economy. Whether you're looking for supplemental income, exploring new career paths, or transitioning to full-time freelancing, clear goals will guide your efforts.

## 5. Understand Market Rates and Pricing:

- Research market rates for your skills and services. Price your offerings competitively while considering your expertise and the value you bring to clients. Transparency in pricing enhances your credibility and attracts clients looking for quality work.

## 6. Create a Diversified Portfolio:

- Diversify your gig portfolio to mitigate risks associated with relying on a single income source. Offer a variety of services or explore gigs in different sectors to ensure stability and adaptability in the ever-changing gig economy.

## 7. Develop Soft Skills:

- Cultivate soft skills such as communication, time management, and adaptability. These skills are crucial in a gig economy where effective collaboration and responsiveness contribute to success.

## 8. Network and Seek Reviews:

  - Actively network within your chosen gig economy community. Seek reviews and testimonials from satisfied clients, as positive feedback enhances your reputation and credibility. Networking can also lead to repeat business and referrals.

## 9. Manage Finances and Taxes:

  - Stay on top of your finances by managing income, expenses, and taxes efficiently. Track your earnings, set aside money for taxes, and explore tools or professional services to simplify financial management.

## 10. Stay Informed and Adapt:

  - Keep yourself informed about changes in the gig economy, market trends, and emerging opportunities. Adaptability is a key trait for success in this dynamic landscape, where staying ahead of the curve can open doors to new and lucrative gigs.

## 11. Balance Work-Life Integration:

- Achieving a healthy work-life balance is crucial in the gig economy. Set boundaries, manage your workload effectively, and prioritize self-care to sustain long-term success.


By following these steps, you can navigate the gig economy strategically and harness its potential for personal and financial growth. The gig economy offers a wealth of opportunities for those who approach it with adaptability, a commitment to continuous improvement, and a proactive mindset.

# CHAPTER 5: MINDSET MATTERS: DEVELOPING A WEALTH-BUILDING MENTALITY

Welcome to the chapter on "Mindset Matters: Developing a Wealth-Building Mentality," where we delve into the transformative power of mindset in the pursuit of financial success. Beyond numbers and strategies, your mindset plays a pivotal role in shaping your relationship with money and influencing your journey towards building wealth.

In this chapter, we explore the psychological aspects of financial success, examining the beliefs, attitudes, and behaviors that can propel you toward your financial goals or hinder your progress. Developing a wealth-building mentality is not just about accumulating monetary assets; it's about cultivating a mindset that fosters financial resilience, adaptability, and a positive relationship with wealth.

We'll unravel the impact of limiting beliefs, explore the principles of abundance thinking, and provide practical insights on how to overcome mental barriers that may be holding you back from reaching your full financial potential. From embracing a growth mindset to understanding the psychology of financial decision-making, this chapter is designed to empower you with the mental tools necessary for sustainable wealth-building.

So, as we embark on this exploration of the intricate interplay between mindset and wealth, be prepared to challenge preconceptions, adopt empowering beliefs, and develop the mental resilience needed to navigate the complexities of personal finance. The journey toward financial success begins in the mind, and by the end of this chapter, you'll be equipped with the insights and strategies to cultivate a mindset that propels you toward lasting prosperity.

# - The Psychology of Wealth

Understanding the psychology of wealth is fundamental to building a strong foundation for financial success. Beyond numbers and financial strategies, our attitudes, beliefs, and behaviors play a crucial role in shaping our financial outcomes. Exploring the psychology of wealth involves delving into the intricate interplay between our thoughts, emotions, and financial decisions. Here are key aspects to consider:

**1. Mindset Matters:**

   - Your mindset, or your deeply ingrained beliefs about money, is a powerful force that influences your financial behavior. The distinction between a fixed mindset (believing that abilities and financial outcomes are static) and a growth mindset (believing that abilities can be developed through dedication and hard work) is particularly relevant. Cultivating a growth mindset opens the door to continuous learning, resilience in the face of challenges, and a willingness to embrace opportunities for financial growth.

## 2. **Abundance vs. Scarcity Thinking:**

- The mindset of abundance versus scarcity profoundly shapes financial decisions. Abundance thinking involves recognizing and appreciating the wealth of opportunities available, fostering a positive outlook on financial endeavors. On the other hand, scarcity thinking is rooted in fear and a belief that resources are limited, potentially leading to risk aversion and missed opportunities.

## 3. **Money Scripts:**

- Money scripts are the unconscious beliefs we hold about money, often formed in childhood based on observations of our parents or caregivers. Identifying and challenging money scripts can be transformative. For example, addressing beliefs such as "money is the root of all evil" or "rich people are greedy" can open the door to healthier financial attitudes.

## 4. Emotional Intelligence in Financial Decision-Making:

- Emotional intelligence plays a critical role in making sound financial decisions. Being aware of your emotions and understanding how they influence your financial behaviors helps you make decisions aligned with your long-term goals. Emotional intelligence also facilitates effective communication about money matters with others, such as family members or financial advisors.

## 5. Delayed Gratification and Patience:

- The ability to delay gratification and practice patience is a hallmark of successful wealth-building. This involves making choices that prioritize long-term financial goals over immediate desires. Developing patience enables individuals to withstand market fluctuations, resist impulsive spending, and stay committed to their financial plans.

## 6. Risk Tolerance and Risk Aversion:

- Understanding your risk tolerance is crucial in investment decisions. Some individuals thrive on risk and seek high-reward opportunities, while others are risk-averse and prefer stability. Balancing risk and reward involves aligning your investment strategy with your comfort level and financial goals.

## 7. Financial Self-Efficacy:

- Financial self-efficacy, or the belief in one's ability to achieve financial goals, is a key determinant of financial success. Fostering a sense of competence and empowerment in financial matters positively impacts behavior, encouraging individuals to take proactive steps toward wealth-building.

**73 | 10 TIPS FOR BUILDING WEALTH IN YOUR 20S**

## 8. **Lifestyle Inflation and Hedonic Adaptation:**

- Understanding the concepts of lifestyle inflation (increasing spending as income rises) and hedonic adaptation (the tendency to return to a baseline level of happiness despite positive or negative changes) helps individuals make conscious choices about spending and lifestyle. Avoiding unnecessary inflation and adapting to circumstances mindfully contribute to financial well-being.

In essence, the psychology of wealth is a dynamic and multifaceted aspect of personal finance. By cultivating a positive mindset, challenging limiting beliefs, and developing emotional intelligence, individuals can align their mental frameworks with their financial goals. Recognizing the psychological factors at play empowers individuals to make informed, intentional decisions that contribute to lasting financial success.

# - Cultivating Healthy Financial Habits

Cultivating healthy financial habits is the cornerstone of building a secure and prosperous financial future. Just as physical health requires consistent exercise and a balanced diet, financial health is nurtured through disciplined and mindful financial practices. Here's a comprehensive guide to help you cultivate and sustain healthy financial habits:

1. **Create a Budget:**

   - Start by creating a realistic and detailed budget that outlines your income, expenses, and savings goals. A budget serves as a roadmap for your finances, helping you allocate resources effectively and avoid unnecessary debt.

2. **Live Below Your Means:**

   - Embrace a lifestyle that allows you to live below your means. While earning more is advantageous, spending less than you earn is the key to financial stability. This practice creates a surplus that can be directed towards savings and investments.

### 3. **Build an Emergency Fund:**

- Establish an emergency fund to cover unexpected expenses and provide a financial safety net. Aim to save three to six months' worth of living expenses in this fund. This ensures you're prepared for unforeseen challenges without disrupting your long-term financial goals.

### 4. **Automate Savings and Investments:**

- Automate your savings and investments to ensure consistency. Set up automatic transfers to your savings account and contribute regularly to investment accounts, such as retirement funds or brokerage accounts. Automation promotes financial discipline and helps you stay on track.

### 5. **Prioritize High-Interest Debt Repayment:**

- If you have high-interest debts, prioritize their repayment. Focus on credit card debt, personal loans, or any other high-interest obligations. Paying off high-interest debt promptly frees up resources for other financial goals.

## 6. Establish Financial Goals:

- Define short-term and long-term financial goals. Whether it's saving for a vacation, buying a home, or planning for retirement, clear goals provide direction and motivation. Break down larger goals into smaller, manageable milestones for a sense of accomplishment along the way.

## 7. Diversify Investments and Retirement Savings:

- Diversify your investments to manage risk and optimize returns. Explore different asset classes, such as stocks, bonds, and real estate. Additionally, regularly review and adjust your retirement savings strategy based on your financial goals and market conditions.

## 8. Practice Mindful Spending:

- Adopt mindful spending habits by distinguishing between needs and wants. Before making a purchase, consider its necessity and its alignment with your financial goals. Mindful spending empowers you to make intentional choices that support your financial well-being.

## 9. Regularly Review Your Finances:

- Set aside time regularly to review your financial situation. This includes monitoring your budget, tracking expenses, and assessing the performance of your investments. Regular financial check-ins help you identify areas for improvement and celebrate progress.

## 10. Educate Yourself About Personal Finance:

- Invest time in educating yourself about personal finance. Stay informed about financial concepts, investment strategies, and market trends. Financial literacy empowers you to make informed decisions and adapt to changes in the economic landscape.

## 11. Seek Professional Guidance:

- Consider seeking professional financial guidance when needed. Financial advisors can provide personalized insights, assist with goal setting, and offer strategies to optimize your financial plan. Their expertise can be valuable in navigating complex financial decisions.

Cultivating healthy financial habits is a continuous process that requires commitment and mindfulness. By integrating these practices into your daily life, you lay the groundwork for financial resilience, long-term stability, and the realization of your financial aspirations. Remember, small, consistent steps lead to significant financial achievements over time.

# - Overcoming Common Mental Barriers to Financial Success

Achieving financial success goes beyond budgets and investment strategies; it involves navigating and overcoming common mental barriers that may hinder progress. Identifying and dismantling these barriers is essential for cultivating a mindset conducive to prosperity. Here's a comprehensive guide to help you overcome mental barriers to financial success:

## 1. **Identify Limiting Beliefs:**

- Begin by identifying any limiting beliefs you may hold about money. These beliefs, often ingrained from childhood or societal influences, can shape your financial decisions. Common limiting beliefs include "money is the root of all evil" or "I'll never be good with money." Recognizing and acknowledging these beliefs is the first step toward overcoming them.

## 2. **Cultivate a Growth Mindset:**

- Embrace a growth mindset, believing that your financial abilities can be developed through learning and effort. A fixed mindset assumes that financial success is predetermined, while a growth mindset acknowledges the potential for improvement and resilience in the face of challenges.

## 3. **Challenge Scarcity Thinking:**

   - Shift from a mindset of scarcity, which focuses on limitations and fears of not having enough, to one of abundance. Abundance thinking acknowledges the wealth of opportunities available and fosters a positive outlook on financial endeavors.

## 4. **Address Fear of Failure:**

   - Fear of failure can paralyze financial decision-making. Instead of viewing setbacks as failures, reframe them as learning opportunities. Understand that setbacks are a natural part of the journey and can provide valuable lessons for future success.

## 5. **Combat Imposter Syndrome:**

   - Imposter syndrome, the feeling of inadequacy or undeserving success, can hinder financial confidence. Acknowledge your accomplishments, skills, and the value you bring to the table. Celebrate your successes and recognize your worth in financial endeavors.

## 6. **Challenge the Fear of Success:**

- Some individuals fear success as much as failure. Success may bring new responsibilities, expectations, or changes in lifestyle. By acknowledging and addressing the fear of success, you can open yourself up to the positive transformations that financial success can bring.

## 7. **Embrace Risk with Informed Decision-Making:**

- Fear of financial risk can lead to missed opportunities. Instead of avoiding risk altogether, educate yourself about potential risks and rewards. Make informed decisions based on your risk tolerance and financial goals, recognizing that calculated risks can lead to financial growth.

## 8. **Address Money Shame:**

- Money shame, stemming from past financial mistakes or societal stigma, can impact financial well-being. Face any feelings of shame, forgive yourself for past errors, and focus on building a positive relationship with money moving forward.

9. **Visualize Financial Success:**

- Use visualization techniques to picture your financial success. Envision your goals being achieved, whether it's paying off debt, buying a home, or reaching a specific level of financial independence. Visualization can reinforce positive beliefs and motivate action.

10. **Seek Support and Education:**

- Don't hesitate to seek support and education. Engage with financial communities, attend workshops, or consult with financial professionals. Surrounding yourself with positive influences and gaining knowledge can bolster your confidence and resilience.

11. **Practice Self-Compassion:**

- Be compassionate with yourself on your financial journey. Understand that everyone makes mistakes, and financial success is a process. Treat yourself with the same kindness you would offer a friend facing financial challenges.

By actively addressing these mental barriers, you empower yourself to build a healthier mindset and make sound financial decisions. Overcoming these obstacles is an ongoing process, and with persistence and self-awareness, you can break free from limiting beliefs and pave the way for lasting financial success.

# CONCLUSION

As we reach the end of "10 Tips for Building Wealth in Your 20s," I hope this journey through the realms of personal finance has been enlightening and empowering for you. Building wealth is not just about accumulating money; it's about cultivating a mindset, adopting healthy habits, and making informed decisions that set the stage for a prosperous future.

In your 20s, you stand at a crucial crossroads where the choices you make can have a profound impact on your financial trajectory. The tips shared in this book are not mere guidelines but rather a blueprint designed to guide you through the intricacies of wealth-building during this pivotal decade of your life.

We've explored the foundations of financial literacy, from understanding budgeting basics and managing debt to investing wisely and navigating the gig economy. Along the way, we've emphasized the importance of mindset, breaking free from limiting beliefs and fostering a growth-oriented approach that propels you toward your goals.

Remember, building wealth is a journey, not a destination. It requires discipline, adaptability, and a commitment to lifelong learning. Each tip in this book serves as a building block, contributing to the construction of your financial future.

As you move forward, embrace the opportunities to diversify your income, invest strategically, and leverage technology for financial growth. Seek out knowledge, surround yourself with a supportive financial community, and continuously assess and adjust your financial plans.

Your 20s are a time of exploration, growth, and laying the groundwork for the decades ahead. By implementing the insights from this book, you've equipped yourself with valuable tools to navigate the complexities of personal finance successfully.

I encourage you to be proactive in your financial journey, to dream big, and to take calculated risks. Remember that wealth is not just about the numbers in your bank account; it's about the freedom to live life on your terms, pursue your passions, and create a future filled with financial security and abundance.

As you step into the future, may the principles shared in these pages guide you, inspire you, and empower you to build the wealth and the life you envision. Here's to a future filled with financial success and fulfilment in every aspect of your journey.

www.ingramcontent.com/pod-product-compliance
Lightning Source LLC
Chambersburg PA
CBHW070029260726
48658CB00002B/551